Interjections

written by Ann Heinrichs

illustrated by Dan McGeehan and David Moore

The Child's World®

Published by The Child's World®
1980 Lookout Drive • Mankato, MN 56003-1705
800-599-READ • www.childsworld.com

ACKNOWLEDGMENTS
The Child's World®: Mary Berendes, Publishing Director
The Design Lab: Design and page production
Red Line Editorial: Editorial direction

LIBRARY OF CONGRESS CATALOGING-IN-PUBLICATION DATA
Heinrichs, Ann.
  Interjections / by Ann Heinrichs ; illustrated by Dan McGeehan and David Moore.
    p. cm.
  Includes bibliographical references and index.
  ISBN 978-1-60253-428-5 (library bound : alk. paper)
  1. English language—Interjections—Juvenile literature. I. McGeehan, Dan, ill. II. Moore, David, ill. III. Title.
  PE1355.H4463 2010
  428.2—dc22   2010011458

Printed in the United States of America in Mankato, Minnesota.
February 2011
PA02095

ABOUT THE AUTHOR

Ann Heinrichs was lucky. Every year from grade three through grade eight, she had a big, fat grammar textbook and a grammar workbook. She feels that this prepared her for life. She is now the author of more than 100 books for children and young adults. She has also enjoyed successful careers as a children's book editor and an advertising copywriter. Ann grew up in Fort Smith, Arkansas, and lives in Chicago, Illinois.

ABOUT THE ILLUSTRATORS

Dan McGeehan spent his younger years as an actor, author, playwright, cartoonist, editor, and even as a casket maker. Now he spends his days drawing little monsters!

David Moore is an illustration instructor at a university who loves painting and flying airplanes. Watching his youngest daughter draw inspires David to illustrate children's books.

Drat!

TABLE OF CONTENTS

What Is an Interjection?

Yahoo!

Ouch!

Yuk!

Wow!

Yum!

These words are **interjections**! Can you imagine life without them? You'd have lots of trouble saying how you feel. Interjections are words you use to get attention or share feelings.

You say some interjections when you are happy, sad, or surprised.

Yippee! It is party time!

Eek! There's a mouse under my chair!

Some interjections are cheers.

Hurray! We finally won!

Bravo! You did a great job!

Some interjections are greetings or good-byes.

Hi, Sarah. How's your monkey?

So long, Bart.

And some interjections just fill up space!

Interjections might have been the earliest human speech. Imagine **prehistoric** people. They might have spoken with grunts and shouts. They might have said things that meant Hey! or Whoopee! or Wow!

Our speech has changed a lot since then, but we still need interjections. Let's check it out!

Words That Stand Alone

Interjections are not like any other part of a sentence. They don't describe anything. They don't name anything. They're not action words. And they don't join words together. They just stand alone.

When you are speaking, it's easy to make an interjection stand alone. Often you just say the interjection and stop. Sometimes you pause a little and then go on.

What about when you're writing interjections? You need to show what your voice would do if you were speaking. You do that with **punctuation marks**.

You can often spot an interjection. Look for the punctuation around it.

Maybe you're excited. Maybe you're angry. Strong interjections show strong feelings. They are followed by an **exclamation point** (!).

Oops! My monkey jumped off its perch.

Hey! Get that monkey off my head!

Some interjections are calmer and quieter. They're called mild interjections. Mild interjections are set off by **commas** (,).

Say, do you have any bananas for my monkey?

No, we have no bananas today.

Well, when will you have bananas?

Gee, I really don't know.

Wait! Stop! It's a Verb!

Exclamation points are good clues for finding interjections. However, not every exclamation point comes after an interjection.

Wait!

Stop!

Help!

Run!

Stay!

All these words have exclamation points. They stand alone. But watch out! They're not interjections. They're really **verbs**.

These words are action words. These words describe things to do or ways to be. Therefore, they are verbs.

Happy Interjections

Use interjections with surprise, delight, and happy feelings, too. Suppose you just found out you won 100 free pizzas.

Wow!

Golly!

Yahoo!

Hurray!

Gee whiz!

Eat the pizzas. Your interjections might be:

Yum!

Yummy!

Mmm!

To get someone's attention, you say Hey! or maybe Yoo-hoo! Greetings and good-byes have interjections, too:

Hi!   Bye!   Hello!   So long!

Good-bye!

Ha! can mean "Oh boy!" or "See there!" or "I don't believe that." If you had a great idea, you'd say Aha! But if you're laughing, you say Ha-ha!

Ha-ha!

COMICS

Not-So-Happy Interjections

You also say interjections when you're not so happy. Maybe you're shocked or disappointed. Maybe you're annoyed. Maybe you're just plain sad.

Suppose you did your homework, but the dog ate it. Which interjection would you use?

Nuts!

Oh dear!

Darn!

Alas!

If you're scared, unhappy, or just fed up, there are plenty of interjections for you!

Yikes! There's a whole nest of ants!

Ouch! That mosquito bit my leg!

Uh-oh! Sparky turned the garbage can over again.

Yuck! Some broccoli just landed on my ice cream!

Ways to Fill Up Space

Some interjections seem to have no purpose. They just fill up space.

Oh, I thought it was time to go.

Say, where did you put that lizard?

The last time I saw him was, um, Thursday.

Some interjections are just sounds. We use groups of letters to stand for mouth and throat sounds.

Shhh! Be quiet!

Ugh! This baloney sandwich is moldy!

Cartoons are full of great interjections. They make everything more exciting!

Zoom! Whoosh! Wham! Boom!

Ka-boom!

Splat!

Animal Interjections

Animals can't speak in words. They can only make sounds. People have ways to spell animal sounds. Some are bow-wow, meow, quack, honk, moo, oink, cluck-cluck, grr, cockadoodle-doo, and hee-haw. Can you think of any others?

How to Learn More

AT THE LIBRARY

Heller, Ruth. *Fantastic! Wow! and Unreal!: A Book About Interjections and Conjunctions*. New York: Puffin Books, 2000.

McClarnon, Marciann. *Painless Junior Grammar*. Hauppauge, NY: Barron's Educational Series, 2007.

Park, Linda Sue. *Yum! Yuck! A Foldout Book of People Sounds*. Watertown, MA: Charlesbridge, 2005.

Schoolhouse Rock: Grammar Classroom Edition. Dir. Tom Warburton. Interactive DVD. Walt Disney, 2007.

ON THE WEB

Visit our home page for lots of links about grammar: *childsworld.com/links*

NOTE TO PARENTS, TEACHERS AND LIBRARIANS: We routinely check our Web links to make sure they're safe, active sites—so encourage your readers to check them out!

Glossary

commas (KOM-uhs): Punctuation marks that break up parts of a sentence. You use commas to set off some interjections.

exclamation point (ek-skluh-MAY-shun POINT): A punctuation mark that comes at the end of a sentence and shows surprise. Exclamation points come after some interjections.

interjections (in-tur-JEK-shuns): Words that get attention or shows feeling and stand alone in a sentence. *Hello!* and *Wow!* are interjections.

prehistoric (pre-hi-STOR-ik): From a time before history was written. Prehistoric people probably used interjections.

punctuation marks (pungk-choo-AY-shun MARKS): Written marks that make the meaning of a sentence clearer. Commas and exclamation points are punctuation marks.

verbs (VURBS): Action words that describe things to do or ways to be. *Run* and *help* are both verbs.

Index